THE BOOK OF THE CHASTE

Ish'dnah

Bishop of Basrah

Translated by: D.P. Curtin

THE BOOK OF THE CHASTE

Copyright @ 2021 Dalcassian Press

All rights reserved. No part of this publication may be reproduced, distributed, or transmitted in any form or by any means, including photocopying, recording, or other electronic or mechanical methods, without the prior written permission of the publisher, except in the case of brief quotations embodied in critical reviews and certain other non-commercial uses permitted by copyright law. For permission request, write to Dalcassian Press at dalcassianpublishing at gmail.com

ISBN: 979-8-3302-3117-1 (Paperback)

Library of Congress Control Number:
Author: Curtin, D.P. (1985-)

Printed by Ingram Content Group, 1 Ingram Blvd, La Vergne, Tennessee

First printing edition 2021.

THE BOOK OF THE CHASTE

Ish'dnah, Archbishop of Basrah
From the French translation by: Fr. Jean-Baptiste Chabot

By the virtue of Our Lord Jesus Christ, we begin to write the abbreviated history of all the Fathers who founded convents in the kingdom of the Persians or the Arabs, of all the Fathers who wrote books concerning the monastic institution, of some metropolitan saints and bishops who either founded schools, or wrote on monastic life, or established convents in the eastern region, and of some virtuous secular men and women, who established convents or monasteries — [story] composed by the friend of God Mar Isho'dnah, metropolitan of Perath-Maischan which is Basrah. May Our Lord help us with their prayers. Amen.

1. — First, Saint Mar Eugene, who founded a stream on Mount Ida, in the neighborhood of the city of Nisibis. — His terrestrial family was from the

country of Egypt, from the island of Clysma. This was his way of acting: he stretched a membrane over his face and went down into the sea; he took out pearls which he distributed to the poor. He did this for twenty-five years. He took the monastic habit in the monastery of Abba Pakôm. He came with his companions to Mount Izla, and built an illustrious convent there. Numerous troops of brothers assembled near him. In that time, Mar Jacob was established as the metropolitan of the city of Nisibis. This Mar Jacob built the cathedral church of Nisibis. Mar Eugene also performed many miracles before King Shapor. Here are those of his disciples who built convents and monasteries: Thomas, Mar Taba, Gouria, Gregory, Iwanis, John, Schalita, Elisha, Serapion, Thecla, sister of Mar Eugene, Stratonice, another sister of Mar Eugene, John, Mar Schêri, Barmichael. He died and was buried in martyrdom, next to the church he had built.

2. — Mar John, founded a convent in the country of Beit Zabdai and Qardou. — He was the disciple of Mar Eugene and received the habit from him. He went to live in the neighborhood of Basrah in Beit Zabdai. He performed many miracles. After completing the course of his life, he emigrated to Our Lord. His body was placed in the monastery of the citadel called Halahalah(?). Now, Rabban Gabriel, from the convent of Zarnouqa, came and transported him to this convent.

3. — The saint who founded a convent in the mountain of Dara, and who was called Mar Schêri. — He had also been a disciple of Mar Eugene: his name was Schêri. He came to Nisibis. He was the breadwinner of eighteen brothers. After practicing asceticism for some time, he came to the mountain of Dara and built a famous monastery there. Later, Mar Sabarjesus, metropolitan of Nisibis, enlarged it and made it an illustrious convent.

4. — Saint Mar John, anchorite, under whose name the monastery of Anbar was built near Baghdad. — His earthly family was of the race of the Roman emperors of the house of Constantine, and his father was a senator. He went to find Mar Eugene, made himself his disciple, and received the monastic habit from him. He then departed, traveled through distant regions, [and went] as far as Jerusalem and Scetus. He performed many wonders that surpass all accounts. He died in peace and was buried in his convent. May his prayers protect the miserable writer, the reader and the listeners. Amen.

5. — Saint Mar Schafita, who founded a current in the country of the Kurds and the Zabdeans. — He was of Egyptian origin. He built three churches; then he went to the monastery of Abba Pakôm and received the habit. Then he came to the village of Phanak, in Beit Zabdai. He lived for some time in this place, performed miracles, and died peacefully at the age of ninety-two. He was placed in the church he had built. May his prayer help us. Amen.

6. — Saint Mar Aha, founder of the convent of Zamouqa. — This saint had been a disciple of Mur Eugène. After his death, grace brought Saint Jerusabran from the convent of Izla to this one. He saw the brothers deprived of water: he prayed, and through his prayer, a spring of water gushed out from under the foundations of the church.

7. — Mar John, who founded the monastery of Kamoul. — His family, which was from Beit Garmai, professed Magism (Zoroastianism) and was pagan; she was descended from the royal race of the Persians. He came to Isisibe and was instructed by Saint Mar Eugene. Then he went to the place where the ark had stopped, and remained there for some time. He died in peace, and was placed in his cave. After a certain period of time, the blessed Rabban Oukama came from the monastery of Mar Abraham the Great, built a magnificent church under the name of Mar John, and placed his body in this church. May their prayers be for the help of the sinful writer, the reader and the listeners. Amen.

8. — Saint Mar Aitalaha, schools of the country of Nouliadran. — He lived in the time of King Shapor. He was accused before him; They threw him in chains and took him to the city of Arbela. He remained there for a long time and was subjected to all the torments. From there they took him to the country of Beit Nouhadra, to the village called Rastegerd, and there they stoned him. In the place where he was stoned a myrtle tree grew; but the pagans, moved by hatred, tore it away. Subsequently, the faithful built a superb monastery under the name of the blessed.

9. — Blessed Bar-Sahde, who built a convent near Harhê, a town located on the Tigris. — He was of Persian origin, from the city of King Shapor. The name of his country was Astahr, and his city was called Hèh-Scliabhour, from the name of the king who built it. He came to the city of Baçrah, and was educated in the

schools. He received the monastic habit. A companion named Sergnifi attached himself to him. He lived ninety years and died in a happy old age, in Tau 128 of the Arabs, on Friday the 5th of Kanoun second. His body was placed in the convent he had founded near the town of Harbê.

10. — Blessed Mar John de Kaschkar, of the monastery of Ain-Deole, on Mount Aroui, in the country of Beit Garmai. — His family was from the country of Kaschkar. After having studied the doctrine of the books, he went to a convent in the country of Kaschkar, the one which was later restored by Saint Mar Gani, disciple of Mar Abraham the Great, and which is still called today by his name. He served in the sanctuary, and was its porter, when, on Resurrection Sunday, he was transported with another ascetic to the desert of Scetus. There he saw the assembly of the anchorites of Beit Onesimos, and received their blessing. The superior of these holy personages ordered him to go and serve at the altar of the Lord in the convent of Ain-Déqla, and the same day he was transported and arrived at the monastery in Beit Garmai. After serving for some time, he died in deep old age and was laid to rest in the sanctuary where he had served, on the 24th of A.D. We commemorate him on the first of tishri.

11. — The martyr Mar Qardag, under whose name convents were built. — By his origin he was from the Persian tribe of Beit Nemroud. His father was one of King Shapor's greats. He was a valiant man in battle and his residence was in the city of Arbela. He built himself a fortress in the neighborhood of Arbela, on a high hill called Malqai. He was instructed by Mar Ebedjesus. He was stoned to death at the gate of the citadel he had built. An important monastery was built here. May his prayer preserve us all. Amen

12. — Saint Mar Gregory, superior, who wrote a book on monastic life. — He was of Persian origin, and was a merchant. He had great visions, and embraced the monastic state. He went to Edessa, and learned from Doctor Moses. From there he came to Mount Izla and remained there in solitude for a long time. He then went to his country and brought his sister to a convent in Nisibis, then he returned to his solitude. He then went to the island of Cyprus, where he became a gardener. He recited all the [holy] books by heart; and he had revelations of all kinds. He finally returned to Mount Izla and, a few days later,

he emigrated to Our Lord in profound old age. He was placed near the shrine of Mar Eugene. May his prayer help us.

13. — Saint Mar Pethion, martyr, and monk of Halwan. — There was a pagan, named Yazdin, who studied the Christian doctrine and went to Karka-of-Beit-Selouk where he learned in the schools. He had a nephew named Pethion. Yazdin brought Pethion who became his disciple. He remained in the mountain for a long time. They preached to the pagans and suffered torture from them. His coronation happened on the 25th of tischri.

14. Saint Mar Abraham the Great, the prince of monks, who founded a convent on Mount Izla in the neighborhood of Nisibis. — His family was from the country of Kaschkar. From his childhood his parents sent him to their village schools. Later he went to the town of Hirta. He preached much among the pagans. He went as far as Egypt, Scetus, and Mount Sinai, then he returned to the schools of Nisibis. He was the companion of Mar Abraham, disciple of Mar Narsai and of John of Beit Rabban, his relative. He performed wonders like the Apostles and he established suitable rules for the monks. He was the first to institute monastic tonsure. Many disciples attached themselves to him, who in turn founded famous convents. Among others: Abba Simeon who founded a convent in the town of Schena; Abba Bar-Idta, in Marga; Georges founded two convents: one in the country of Marga, and the other near the village of Roumain; .Mur Babai of Nisibis, who founded a convent on Mount Izla; Rabban SahrawaJ who founded a convent in the Qardou mountains; Henanjesus who founded a convent in the mountain of Dîbôr and Salak, and Mar Abba, his master; Mar Yônan, who laid the foundations of the Bar-Toura monastery; Mar Jacob, who founded the monastery [of Hebischa; Mar Sabarjesus, who founded the convent of] Aba Schapîrfi, in the region of Beit Nouhadra; Mar Yônan, the slave, who founded a convent in the country of Adiabene near Ashgar; Rabban Sabôkt, who built a monastery in the mountain of Singar; Daniel, who founded a convent in the mountain of Orouk, at a place called Baçlawi; Mar Schalita, who founded a convent in the mountain of Haran; Mar Gani, who founded a convent in Beit Aramayê, in the country of Kaschkar; Rabban Mar Oukama, who restored the cave of Mar John de Kamoul and made it a convent; Mar Yôna, from the convent of Ghelala in the country of Qardou; Jesusabran, who built the convent of Zarnouqa in the country of Herat; Mar John, who founded the convent of Nehel in the country

of Arzoun; saint Bar Kêwêla, who fought against the heretics and founded the great church of the city of Kephar-Touta; Mar Babai the Great, who also founded a famous monastery in Beit Zabdai; Rabban John, called Adarmah, who built a convent in the country of Dasen; Mar Elia and Henanjesus who left the monastery of Mar Abraham and founded [convents; Mar Joseph, who founded] the convent of Samarouna; George, who founded a convent in the desert of the town of Merw. These are the spiritual sons of Abraham of Kaschkar who founded convents in these regions, as well as Abraham of Nethpar, Mar Job and Stephen; and I will tell their story successively. — After some time he returned his holy soul to Our Lord, at the age of eighty-five years, and they placed his holy body in the church which he had erected. May his prayers and those of his children be a protective wall for the sinning writer, for his brothers and his parents. Amen.

15. — Saint Bar-'Idta, who founded a convent in the mountain of Marga. — His family was from the land of Nineveh; from his youth he studied books and attended the schools of Nisibis.

He made progress in all the doctrine of the Church and in the Greek sciences. Having found Rabban Mar Abraham of Kaschkar in the school, he attached himself to him and became his spiritual son and his disciple. He went up to Mount Izla, where he remained for some time and was the firstborn of the disciples of Mar Abraham. When his master left this temporal life, he came to the land of Marga and dwelt in the western region. He built a famous convent, and more than four hundred brothers gathered around him. Among those who came to receive the habit from him were: Abba Simeon, who founded a convent in the town of Schena, in the mountains near the Tigris; Rabban Mar Yozedek, [who founded a convent in the country of Qardou; Rabban Hormizd], who founded a convent on the mountain of Beit 'Adrai; John the Persian who built the convent of Ghelala, in the country of Qardou, at the foot of the mountain. — After working for many years, he emigrated to Our Lord in a happy old age. It is commemorated on the first Sunday of the Dedication.

16. — Saint Mar Georges who founded two convents: one in the country of Adiabène around the village of Roumîni(?), and the other in the country of Marga. — [...] there they separated. He went to live in a cave in the mountain of Adiabene, in the village of [Rou]minis(?). Later he built a famous convent,

and about fifty men gathered near him. He preached in the country of Biarga and Babagasch, and [established] a famous convent in the village of Birta, in the country of Marga, at a place called Beit Zaitê. Rabban Basima, who founded a monastery in the country of Qardou, came to find him, received the habit from him, and was directed by him. Adorned with all virtues, he migrated to his Lord.

17. — Mar Babai of Nisibis, who founded a monastery on Mount Lela. — He was from the city of Nisibis, descendant of those Persians who King Shapor had brought and established in this city. He went to Mar Abraham, made himself his disciple and devoted himself to asceticism under his direction. After the death of his master, he put on a worn cloak and went to the mountain of Adiabene. He settled in a cave near the village of Ati, between Beit Gamala and the town of Aschgar, where Mar Abda lived with him, who subsequently founded a convent in this very place. He went to receive the life-giving mysteries in the convent of Mar Jesuszeka - the one who cast out a demon from Na'aman, king of Hirta, with the catholicos Sabarjesus - then he returned to his home. Later, following a divine revelation, he went to Mount Izla, and built a convent in an ancient ruined monastery. He emigrated to Our Lord at the age of seventy-five and his sacred body was placed in front of the balustrade of the altar, in the northern part of the building. May his prayer be of help to the sinful writer.

18. — Saint Mar Sahrawai. — This one also went to Mar Abraham and made himself his disciple. His family was from Nisibis. After the death of his master, he went to the country of Qardou; he built there and decorated a convent. He performed many miracles. After having enjoyed a profound old age, he emigrated to Our Lord and was deposited in the church which he had built. This convent is called Sa'id monastery,

19. — Mar Elias, who founded a monastery in the mountains of Mosul. — He was originally from Hirta, a city of the Arabs. After having studied ecclesiastical sciences in the church of his village, he went with great eagerness near Mar Abraham, at Mount Izla, and took the monastic habit. He then left and came to Mosul. He went up to a nearby mountain, and lived in solitude there. When the number of brothers increased, Mar Elias built a church. He performed wonders like the Apostles. He migrated to his Lord when he was over a

hundred years old. He was placed in the small martyrion that he had built. May his prayer [protect] the sinful writer.

20. — Saint John of Adarmai, who founded a convent in the country of Dascn. — His family was from Beit Aramayè, from the country of Kaschkar. He went to Mar Abraham and became his disciple. When his master died, he left the monastery with the blessed George and Abba Bar-Idta, and they came to the country of Marga. From there grace called him to go to the country of Dasen, where he built a magnificent church. Brothers gathered around him and, after having endured the passion of Christ, he emigrated to Our Lord, and his body was placed in the martyrdom which he had built.

21. — Saint Mar Henanjesus, who founded a convent in the country of Salak and Dîbôr. — He was of Ismaili origin, from the family of King Na'aman. He went to Mar Abraham at his monastery. He attached himself to Mar Babai the Great, to Mar Elias, his relative, and to George the martyr, who was descended from the race of Khosrau, king of the Persians. He adopted the habit and settled in a cave. He engaged in great controversy with the heretics. He then went to the country of Dîbôr and Salak, and began to preach. He lived another twenty years after building the convent, and died in a happy old age. He was placed in the church he had built.

22. — Saint Mar John, who founded, in the country of Artoun, a convent which is called the convent of Nehel [...] — After the death of his master Mar Abraham, he left the convent where he no longer enjoyed peace because of the dissension which existed among the brothers, and he came to the country of Arzoun. Two brothers accompanied him. When they reached the mountain near the village of Nehel, he settled there in solitude. He built a convent in a place neighboring Nehel, which had previously been a monastery. temple of idols, after having enjoyed a profound old age he left the temporal life, and his body was placed in the church which he had built.

23. — Saint Mar John, founder of the monastery of Qanqal. —At the time when Mar Babai the Great was in his monastery, this saint came to him and placed himself under his direction. He stayed near him for some time. Then he went to. Jerusalem and Scetus, and settled in the city of Emesa. For two years, he took care of the shrine [containing] the head of John the Baptist; then he

was ordained priest by the bishop of Emesa. After the death of the bishop, another bishop was ordained. A discord arose between him and the bishop, because the faithful honored him more than the bishop. He came to the town of Arzoun, on the bank of the river Sarbat, near the village called Qanqal. He had many disciples. Mar John the Baptist appeared to him in a dream and said to him: "Return to Emesa; go to the place where my reliquary is, take a relic of the hair of my head, I will give it to you myself, and come back and build yourself a convent in this place." He went as he had been told in this dream, took the hair that the saint had given him, and returned to build a famous monastery. He placed the hair in the eastern foundation of the altar. As the time of his death approached, he called his [spiritual] children and ordered them to place his body at the door of the church outside, so that whoever came in or out would trample it under foot, and that by humility He emigrated to Our Lord the first from first Kanoun, and his children left him at the door of the church, as he had ordered. May his prayer help the sinful writer.

24. — Saint Mar Jacob, who founded the convent of Hebîscha, in the neighborhood of Arzoun, near the town of Seert. — He received the habit of certain anchorites who inhabited the Qardou mountains. He went to find Saint Mar Hebîscha, and stayed with him for a long time. They both participated in the erection of the convent. Mar Tyris, bishop of Mahôzê de Arzoun of Beit Garmai, mentions this saint Mar Hebîscha in the first part of his book on monastic life. After shining with their faith, they migrated to their Lord and were deposited in the temple which they had built. May their prayers be for the help of the sinful writer.

25. — Saint Mar Aba, who first laid the foundations of the monastery of Bar-Toura, which was then completed by Abba Yônan, his disciple. — The family of Saint Mar Aba was from the country of Beit'Arabayê, from the village called Hôrdepna; he was a fellow citizen of the righteous Mar Gabrouna who founded the monastery of Schamouna, in the mountain of Pirdoun, on the borders of [Beit] Zabdai and [Beit] Arabayê. At the age of twelve, he went to find Saint Mar Dadjesus, disciple of Mar Abraham the Great, who lived in the mountain of Abiabene, and he stayed with him for some time. He then returned to the monastery of Mar Abraham, in Izla, received the holy habit, and there devoted himself to asceticism. Two brothers attached themselves to him: Gabriel and Berikjesus, as well as another named Oukama. Rabban

Oukama was appointed bishop of Arzoun. In his old age, brothers joined him, and he came to build the monastery of Kamoul, in the country of Qardou. In this place he left temporal life. Mar Gabriel and Berikjesus came to live in the mountains of Singar. By the care of Mar Aba, a small church was built in the place called Bar-Toura. Then came Mar Yônan. He was the man sent by God to turn this place into a famous convent and to be the [spiritual] father of many monks. Mar Aba never stopped lavishing him with advice. He ended his journey in a happy old age and emigrated to Our Lord. He was placed in the little church he had built.

26. — Mar Sabarjesus, who founded the convent of Abu Schapira. — Blessed Sabarjesus was from the land of Nineveh. He went to the town of Arbele, where he studied books. He heard about Mar Abraham the Great, went to him, made himself his disciple, and stayed with him for some time. Then, grace called him to go build a convent in the country of Beit Nouhadra. Sabarjésus was one of the brothers who [left] the Great Convent with Mar George the Martyr. After having practiced all the virtues, he emigrated to Our Lord, and his body was placed in the convent that he had built. Later, Mar Schou[bhalmaran] came to this place and made known his virtues in the convent of Mar Sabarjesus. Saint Mar Babban Afnimaran also illustrated this convent with all kinds of virtues.

27. — Saint Mar Yânan, who founded a convent in Diabene. — This blessed one belonged to a magus from the village of Pharôk-Abad in Adiabene. One day when he was sent to the village of Ashgar to bring back wine from his master's vineyard, he happened to pass near the cave of Saint Mar Babai of Nisibis. — After the death of Mar Abraham, Mar Babai left the monastery and came to live in the mountain of Adiabene, in the vicinity of the village of Ati-of-Beit-Gamala, as the history of Mar Yônan shows. He turned away from his path and went near Saint Mar Babai. Because of his affection for the saint's way of life, he was filled with ardor by the words of Saint Mar Babai. As the day drew to a close, he could no longer go to the village to load the wine, and he feared being frowned upon by his master, Mar Babai took pity on him and said to him: "Fill the skins with the water of my fountain and load them on your donkey; pour these skins of water into the vessels of your master, and do not be afraid." So he filled the skins with water and went away He met his master who came to taste the wine he brought back While he was seized with great terror,

fearing that his master would mistreat him and incriminate him, by the prayers of Mar Babai the water was changed into a wine which by its sweetness and its excellence aroused the astonishment of the magician himself Having learned of the miracle which had taken place, he went to find Mar Babai in his cave, and implored his prayer. On the orders of the saint, he freed Yônan. made progress in the fear of God, he returned to the mountain of Adiabene to Mar Babai, whose spiritual son and disciple he became. Some time later, he built a convent in this place which he decorated magnificently. After a happy old age, rejoicing in the many spiritual sons he had fathered, he emigrated to Our Lord and his body was placed in the convent he had built. May his prayer come to the aid of the sinful writer.

28. — Mar Gani, who founded a convent in the country of Kaschkcar. — This blessed one was from Beit-Aramaye, from the blessed country of Kaschkar. He was a man rich in herds, in slaves and in servants: he distributed his wealth to the poor and went to the convent of Izla, near Mar Abraham, and received from him the holy habit. He took with him one of his servants who also took the holy habit of monasticism. After the death of Mar Abraham he went to Jerusalem, Scetus and Mount Sinai. He then returned to his country of Kaschkar, and his servant with him. Saint Mar Simeon of Taiboutha, also called Lucas, bears witness to Mar Gani and recounts his virtues. Saint Mar Gani said that it is not permitted for monks to talk together before the time of Tierce. He built a convent in the desert plain of the country of Caschkar. He emigrated to Our Lord and his body was placed in the convent that he had built.

29. — Saint Mar Sabâkt, disciple of Mur Abraham of Izla, who founded a monastery in the mountain, near the town of Singar. — This blessed one was from the city of Nisibis, the son of noble and rich people. Sabôkt went up with Sahrawai to Mar Abraham and received the monastic habit from him. He attached himself to Mar Babai of Nisibis. When Mar Abraham died, he joined the holy followers of Mar Aba, Gabriel and Berikjesus who laid the first foundations of the convent of Bar-Toura and lived there in solitude. He himself built an important convent above Bar-Toura. After practicing virtue, he emigrated to Our Lord on Confessors' Friday, and his body was placed in the martyrion that he had built. May his prayer help the sinful writer.

30. — Saint Mar Oukama, who founded a convent in the cave of Mar John of Kamoul, a village in the country of Qardou. — First the heaven said: "With me [are] the kingdom and the angels"; and the earth answered him saying: "With me [are] the assemblies of the righteous". Heaven says: "With me the angels who stand before the throne"; the earth says: "With me the peoples and nations innumerable who stand before the Cross". The sky says: "With me the stars and the stars"; the earth says: "With me the just and the humble." The sky says: "At home the thunder which make your inhabitants tremble, the earth says: "At home the prayers which inspire fear in yours". The sky says: "At home the thunderbolts which descend on you without scale"; the earth says: "Among me are the righteous who fly to you without wings." Heaven says: "Among me are the clouds that carry rain without fountains"; the earth says: "With me the Virgin who conceived without a man". The sky says: "With me the dew which spreads its blessing everywhere", the earth says: "With me the tears which appease the God of gods". The sky says: "With me the angels who scatter the clouds"; the earth says: "With me the saints who revive the dead". Heaven says: "With me the flames which consume the wicked"; the earth says: "With me the baptism which blots out sins". The sky says: "With me the fire which burns the ungodly"; the earth says: "With me the Sacrifice which quickens those who eat it". The sky says: "I have honored my Master, and I have darkened my stars so that the Lord may not be seen on Golgotha"; the earth says: "I have resurrected him, I I trembled and shuddered in my foundations; I opened my tombs, I summoned my dead, I gathered around the Sepulcher those who were buried, I put on black garments and I sat in mourning until I see him resurrecting in glory; and three days later he made me take off my black clothes and put on white clothes". The sky says: "I am the happiness of the saints"; the earth says: "He has taken me from the dust, he has raised me from the ashes; he made me sit at his right; he filled his tables with excellent food and made me eat; he has prepared life in his chalice, and made me drink; he has established the garden of his church with me, and I now await the fulfillment of his joyful promises". Heaven says: "He sits on his throne with me"; the earth says: "With me is his altar". the earth says: "On the day of his resurrection he girded me with a crown". The sky says: "With me the Creator alone is worshiped, and with you, earth, they worship all kinds of idols of silver and gold"; the earth says: "If there are among me, those who worship the idols, among me also are the martyrs who appease God with their blood."

31. — Mar Daniel, who built a convent in the mountain of Ourouk. — His family was from Beit-Aramaye, from Kaschkar, in the land of Babylon, and his parents were worshipers of idols. This blessed one went near Mar Abraham [...] dahs the mountain of Ourouk and built a monastery there. Having obtained the crown of martyrdom, he emigrated to Our Lord and his body was placed in his monastery. May his prayer come to the aid of the faithful. Amen.

32. — The blessed Mar Bar-Kewela, who founded a church at Kephar-Touta, a city in Mesopotamia. — After the death of Rabban Abraham, Bar-Kewela left the convent and came to the city of Kephar-Touta where he lived in a cave for a certain time. This city was famous for the impiety of Jacob Bourdeana, Severus and Cyril. This is why the heretics constantly went to him, to obtain his support. Many times he asked for a place to build a church without being granted it. He remained there for a long time, in the hope of spreading orthodoxy: many people allowed themselves to be persuaded by his words. He built a magnificent church, in which the office was frequently celebrated. He performed miracles and taught the whole city. He emigrated to Our Lord and his body was placed in the church he had built. May his prayer come to the aid of the faithful. Amen.

33. — Saint Rabban Yôna who founded a convent in the country from Qardou. — His family was it is said [...] of him that his life he does not live from money. After studying the books, he went up at Mount Izla, received the holy habit and dwelt there in solitude. Then, grace led him to the ruined monastery which had once been founded near the village of Houtîr, by a disciple of Mar Eugene. He built a beautiful church and a home for the brothers there. Many brothers gathered near him. At the age of eighty-four, he emigrated to Our Lord and his body was placed in the monastery he had built. May his prayer help the sinful writer!

34. — Saint Mar Jacob founded the monastery of Beit-Aibê in the mountain of Marga. — His family was from Beit-Garmai, from the village of Laschoum. He went diligently to worship some [anchorites] who lived in the mountain. He then attended the schools of the village of Adrayê, and he attached himself to a doctor who was one of the disciples of Mar John de Beit Rabban and who taught him and made him study books. Then he went to the village of Beit Mabar (?) and taught there for some time. He constantly visited Sabarjesus who

then lived in the mountain of Sche'ran and who subsequently became bishop of Laschoum, then catholicos; he lived in his privacy. He went to Jerusalem, made his devotions there and returned to the monastery of Mar Abraham where he took the habit. Later, because of jealousy and some discussion, he left the convent of Mar Abraham with nine brothers who had joined him. Mar Jacob then separated from them and went to the country of Marga, to the north, to a place called Beit-Abê. There were many woods and reeds in this place which had previously been a temple of idols. He built a beautiful church there and the brothers who were with him built cells. Adorned with the crown of old age, he emigrated to Our Lord and his body was placed in the martyrdom that he had built. May his prayer come to the aid of the sinful and miserable writer. Amen.

35. — Saint Mar Schalita, bishop who founded a current between Haran and Edessa. His family was from Beit Grarmai, his village was called Zarak. He went to Mai Abraham [in Izla], received the monastic habit, and there devoted himself to asceticism for some time. He was then established as bishop of Haran, and he built many churches. He built a convent in the mountain of Haran which brought together many brothers. He emigrated to his Lord in a happy old age and was deposited in the convent which he had built. May his prayer protect us all. Amen.

36. — Saint Mar George Marwajsaya, who founded the convent Egalgal in the neighborhood of Merw, town of Khorasan. — He was originally from Persia, his parents were rich. They wanted to have him instructed in the doctrine of the Persians, like the great ones of this world, he did not consent, but he went to the schools of the life-giving doctrine founded in his episcopal city by Saint Bar-Schaba who preached the true faith to the town of Merw. His father asked him: "Why do you not study Persian doctrine?" He replied: "Because any doctrine which does not teach the fear of God is a lie of Satan [...] His father was surprised at what he heard him say. After studying at the schools, he went to Jerusalem and made his devotions to the Holy Places. He then returned to Mount Izla near Mar Abraham, whose disciple he remained, then he returned to his country and lived in the village of Zaraq in a tent that he had erected. In time, brothers gathered around him and he built a monastery with a school. He emigrated. towards Our Lord and was placed in the church which he had built.

37. — Saint Mar Joseph Marwazaya, who founded in the country of Palestine, in the mountain of Ephraim, a convent called the place of Samarouna. — His family was from the famous town of Merw, in the country of Khorasan. He and his parents were owners of wealth. Having heard of the blessed Mar Abraham of Mount Izla, he went to him and received the monastic habit from him; then he went to Jerusalem. He built an illustrious convent. After having distinguished himself by his works of virtue, he emigrated to Our Lord and his body was placed in the church that he had built.

38. — Saint Mar Dadjesus, director and superior of the court ni, disciple of Mar Abraham the Great. — His family was from Beit Aramayw. He abandoned his parents and went to the schools of Nisibis, where he learned. He left there to go to Diabene, and he studied the holy books in the schools of the city of Arbela. Then he went up to the mountain of Adiabene and dwelt there in solitude. When Mar Abraham was about to leave this world, his disciples said to him: "O our Father, to whom are you leaving the convent?" And he answered them: "Dadjesus will come from the mountain of Adiabene and will take charge of the convent. Do not worry". Three months after the death of the old man, Mar Dadjesus came, and directed the convent in a prosperous manner. At the age of seventy-five he passed away, and his body was laid to the south, opposite Mar Abraham.

39. — Saint Mar Babai the Great, who founded a famous school and monastery in Beit Zabdai. — His family was from Beit Zabdai; his village was called Beit 'Ainatha, his parents were faithful, owners of servants and maids. He applied himself to the study of doctrine and commentaries for fifteen years, then he was a doctor at Nisibis in the xenodochion. Later he went to the mountain near Mar Abraham, and made himself his disciple. He remained for some time in this place, then he returned to Beit Zabdai and built in the middle of his parents' fields a famous monastery to which he added large schools. He returned to the monastery of Mar Abraham and lived there in solitude for a long time. He wrote many books and commentaries. He went to Our Lord at the age of seventy-seven years, and his body was placed between Mar Abraham and Mar Dadjesus.

40. — Saint Mur Yab, the ascetic who wrote about God and his creatures. This holy man of God lived on the mountain of Beit Nouhadra, in a place called

Ferîscha. Later he came to Mar Daniel, who lived in the mountain of Uruk, and settled near him. He wrote many books. In profound old age he emigrated to Our Lord and was placed in his cave.

41. — Saint Abimelech, interpreter of treachings, who ran the school at Beit-Sahdê, in Nisibis, at the entrance to the mountain, — This blessed one was from the country of Qardou. He went up to the mountain of Izla and became the disciple of Mar Abraham. He [first] became a doctor in the town of Balad. Then, Mar Elias, metropolitan of Nisibis, forced him to become a doctor and interpreter of the school of Beit Sahdê built by the deacon Elisha. He built the monastery himself with cut stones. He performed many miracles. Adorned with all the virtues, he emigrated to Our Lord, and he was placed in the school monastery.

42. — Saint Mar Abraham, interpreter and martyr of Nisibis. — His family was from the country of Behqawad in the region of the Aramayê. He studied the doctrine in his country; then grace brought him to the city of Nisibis, where he was a doctor for a time. He then went up near Mar Abraham, made himself his disciple and by order of his master became a doctor in the school of Beit Sahdè. One day as he was going to one of the villas of the monastery, a troop of Roman brigands attacked him; one of them struck him with the spear he carried in his hand and he died. The faithful went out, took his body while singing the office and placed it in the school of Beit Sahdê.

43. — Saint Mar Abraham of Nethpar, who wrote on monastic life. — He was from Adiabene, from the village of Beit Nethpar. His parents were faithful family members of the martyrs put to death by King Shapor who shed their blood in the waters of the Dara River, near Beit Nethpar. In his youth he studied books. Then he went to live in a cave two steps away from Beit Nethpar, his village. He stayed there for three years. After that he went to Egypt, to the monastery of Abba Pakomios; then he returned to Adiabene to live in his cave. He wrote many books. He died at a happy old age and was buried in the village church of Beit Nethpar. Sometime later, Mar [Job (?)] built a convent above his cave and transported him there.

44. — Mar Job, who founded a convent in the region of Adiabene. — He was of Persian origin, from the town of Riwardeschir. His parents owned slaves and

servants; his father was a pearl and precious stone merchant. He sent him to the country of the Romans, carrying pearls for the capital. He arrived as far as Nisibis, and lodged in a convent [located] to the east of this city. By an effect of divine providence, he fell seriously ill there. He saw the brothers of this monastery devoted to study and reading, and taking food in the evening until the following evening. Their way of life pleased him. He began to meditate and say to himself: "Where are my ancestors and the kings they served? As for me, I will spend the rest of my life like these monks, if I recover from this disease." In a few days he recovered from his illness; he freed his servants, and learned the divine doctrine, to the point that he read all the books. Then he went to the monastery of Mar Abraham of Nethpar and remained. in this place many brothers gathered around him. In deep old age, he went to Our Lord and his body was placed in the temple that he had built.

45. — Saint Mar Qardag, from the family of Mar Babai the Great. — He was from the country of Ma'alta and Henaita. He studied the Scriptures and the Commentaries in the schools of Beit A founded his village. Bar-Schabta, bishop of the city of Henaita, put him at the head of a monastery for a long time. Then he went to Mar Abraham and became his disciple. He remained in solitude for forty years. He emigrated to our Lord illustrated by works of virtue.

46. — Saint Mar John, from the monastery of Me'are on Mount Lela. — His family was from the town of Hirta, among the Arabs. He was the son of rich and famous parents. He left his city, went to Xisibe, the mother of sciences, and there learned. Then he was a shepherd of flocks in the mountain of Siugar. Then he went to Mount Izla and lived in a place called Me'are. There he experienced many miracles, and after enjoying old age, he emigrated to Our Lord. An Armenian prince whose daughter he had healed wanted to take her body to his country of Armenia; but the local inhabitants opposed it. One of this leader's soldiers had the impiety to cut off the saint's head, and they took him to their country. His body was buried in his cave, and an illustrious temple was built above it which is still called today "monastery of Me'are, of Mar John the Arab".

47. — Saint Mar Jesuszeka, who built three convents and annexed schools to them. — His family was from Schcna, a town in Beit Ramman, called by the Persians Qardil-abad. From his childhood he was instructed in the holy books.

He then went to build a monastery in Beit-Arabaye; and he established teachers and schools in this monastery. Then he went to the mountains of Heftoun and Beit Bagasch. At the time of his old age, he came to the region of Adiabene, leaving his monastery in the hands of the masters as well as the schools which he had annexed there. He built a monastery of stone and lime in a place in the mountains of Adiabene which was more than any other the den of thieves. He established teachers and schools there and, to this day, it is called by his name: "lime monastery (rafa) of Jesuszeka". He went with the catholicos Mar Sabarjesus near Na'aman, king of the Arabs, who lived in the city of Hirta. They healed the king and his disciples. Later, he went to visit Mar Jacob of Beit-Abê. After reaching a great old age, he emigrated to Our Lord, and his body. was deposited in the monastery of the Adiabene mountains, more than two hundred years later, the monastery was devastated. The monks of the monastery of Rabban Yônan, in the mountain of Adiabene, then came to remove the body of Mar Jesuszeka from his monastery. In the third year of the reign of Djaffar, son of Mo'taçem, king of the Arabs. His body was found intact and without corruption after more than two hundred and sixty years. They placed it in a new coffin and placed it near the tomb of blessed Mar Yônan, founder of this holy house.

48. — Blessed Mar Nestorius, who founded a convent in the country of Adiabene. — His family was from the country of Dasen. In his youth, he went to the mountain of Halita (?), near a monk who lived in a cave, and made himself his disciple. He gave him the holy habit, and he worked under his direction in reading books and studying the doctrine. When this monk died, Nestorius buried him in his cave and he himself remained there. As there were many coming and going there, he left this place for the country of Adiabene. Many brothers lived with him, and he built a convent in the vicinity of the village called Raçaf (?). As Mar Babai of Nisibis lived in the mountain of Adiabene, these two characters, Mar Nestorius and Mar Babai, continually enjoyed together the charms of divine conversation. At the age of seventy-three, Mar Xestorius went to Our Lord and was laid to rest in the martyrion he had built.

49. — Saint Abba Yânan, who founded the monastery of Bar-Toura in the vicinity of the town of Singar. — When he was young, an angel appeared to him in a dream [and said to him]: "Get up, go and find Saint Sabôkt and stay

near him in the monastery; copy the manuscripts and learn from books with his spiritual children". He got up, did as he had been told in a dream, and became the spiritual son and disciple of Sabôkt for a certain time. Then he went to find Saint Mar Aba who at that time had left the Great Monastery and was living in. Bar-Toura. He became his servant, and many brothers gathered near them. Mar Aba then said to his children: "Here is the man whose hands will transform this little temple, which we have built to celebrate there. the holy mysteries, in a great and illustrious convent. God chose him so that this building would be placed under his name". He then gave him the monastic habit and taught him the way of the fear of God. He served the brothers for ten years. Mar Aba then died; he placed him in the temple and remained there. Many brothers gathered around him; he built a large temple and cells for the brothers. The saint later left the monastery of Bar-Toura, which he had built, because of the disturbance in the country, and he went with all his spiritual sons to the monastery of the nun Hadoudokt. He said to the brothers: "You will bury me here; but do not let this grieve you. After seven years peace will reign; you will return to the monastery, and I will return there with you". Then he stretched out his feet and died. He was buried in this monastery seven years later. The brothers gathered in the convent of BarToura, and came to the monastery to collect the body of the saint which they placed at the feet of saints Mar Aba and Mar Gabriel.

50. — Saint Bar-Qousrê, who built a monastery in Mosul. — His family was from the land of Nineveh. He applied himself to reading books from his youth. He then went to find Mar Job, disciple of Mar Abraham of Nethpar, who founded a monastery in the region of Adiabene. He gave him the monastic habit and he worked in all humility to serve the brothers. After fifteen years he went to Jerusalem. When he returned, he went up to Mount Elpheph, in the land of Nineveh, and dwelt there in a cave. The heretics who lived in this mountain often mistreated him. He then came to Hesna Ebraya, that is to say Mosul, because at that time the city was not yet built and it was only a very small fortress. Brothers gathered near him and built a monastery and cells. He emigrated to the Lord, adorned with all virtues, on the first Sunday of the Apostles' Fast.

51. — Saint Rabban Gabrouna, who founded in the mountain of Pirdoun (?), that is to say in Qarta (?), a convent which is still called today the convent of Schamouna. — His family was from Beit-Arabaye, from the village of

Hôrdepna. He abandoned his parents and went to find the Fathers who lived in the monastery of Bar-Toura. He devoted himself to asceticism with the spiritual children of Mar Yônan. Then, after a while, he went to the mountain called Pirdoun, on the borders of Beit Zabdai and Beit 'Arabayé, and remained there in solitude. There then existed in the mountain of Pirdoun a fortress whose leader, called Shamouna, had a daughter possessed by the demon: the saint healed her. Brothers gathered near him and he built there at the expense of Shamouna a remarkable temple [which is still called] today by the name of the latter. Adorned with all of the virtues, he emigrated to our Lord, and was deposited in the temple which he had built.

52. — Saint Mar Habib, from the monastery of Qardou. — As soon as he was a youth, he eagerly headed to the schools of the royal city of Ctcaiphon. There he studied and took the habit; then he came to Mount Zinai with thirty pious men from Nineveh. Later, they built a beautiful church on Mount Zaniar. Habib lived in this place for some time. Then he had a vision telling him to go and live in a certain monastery, in the village of Kephar-Touta. Brothers gathered around him and built a remarkable temple. He went to Our Lord at Tagus one hundred and twenty years old, and his body was placed in the temple that he had built.

53. — Saint Mar Basima, from the monastery of Kephar-Touta. — The family was from the country of Qardou. At the age of thirty, he enrolled in the service of the king of the earth, because he was a strong and valiant man. He then had a dream. He mounted a camel and ran to tell it to a magician who said to him: "You will be a monk, according to your own words." Later, he came to Karka from Beit Selouk, and entered the monastery of Mar Çeliba. He learned the doctrine there and then went to find the blessed Mar Georges who had founded two convents, in Marga and in Adiabene. He gave him the habit. After some time, he returned to the country of Qardou and found it. twelve Fathers who lived in the caves of this mountain. He remained with them. He received the order from God to go to the monastery built by Habib. He enlarged and decorated the monastery. He emigrated to Our Lord and was placed at the feet of Saint Mar Habib.

54. — Saint Mar Titus, who built the cathedral church of Hadeth. — He was from the country of Siarzour, from a family of magi. Because of the plague, he

left his country, with his mother, and came to live in Karka-de-Beit Selouk. God then placed in his heart the desire to embrace the life-giving doctrine; and he became the disciple of Doctor Dinhâ. He studied the Scriptures and the sciences, then he went down to Medinat esch-Schaleni, near the Catholicos Mar Ezekiel. He stayed there for some time and received the habit. Then the Catholicos ordained him bishop of the city of Hadeth and wrote to the metropolitan of Assyria to receive him. He gave him a countryside around the city. He performed many wonders and miracles; he fought the heretics and drove them from the city. He then built a beautiful church, and after having fulfilled the functions of the episcopate for some time, he emigrated to Our Lord on the sixth day of first Kanun.

55. — Saint Rabban Schabhour, who founded a monastery in the country of Beit Houzâyê. — He studied books from his childhood and received the holy habit. He carried out propaganda among the pagans and lived in the mountain near the town of Shushtara. He built a magnificent convent in a place which had previously been a temple of idols. Adorned with all the virtues, he emigrated to Our Lord, and his body was placed in the basilica where the office is held during the summer.

56. — Saint Gregory, metropolitan of Nisibis, who wrote on the duties of monastic life, made many proselytes, and built a school. — His family was from Beit-Araniayê, from the blessed country of Kaschkar. His parents were Christians. He remained an orphan. He went to the schools of the royal city of Mahôzê and studied books there. The inhabitants of Arbela came for him and asked him to be a doctor. He was therefore an interpreter and doctor in Arbela for some time; then he went to found a school in Kaschkar. During his time, Eanana the Adiabenian was an interpreter at Nisibis and perverted the faith. The saint having shown mercy towards him, the inhabitants of Arbela looked at him with an evil eye. He fled during the night, cursed the city, and went to the pagans where he preached a lot and wrote books and Ecclesiastical History. Then he returned to Kaschkar, his country, and ended his temporal life there.

57. — Saint Mar George, monk and martyr, founded a school in Babylon, and wrote on monastic life and against heretics. — His family was from Beit-Aramaye, from the country of Babylon. He was a magician, then he embraced the Orthodox faith and received baptism. He went to the Great Monastery,

near Mar Dadjesus, and took the monastic habit. He remained there for some time and wrote books on the duties of monks and against the heretics who followed Gabriel of Singar. Then, through the malice of the inhabitants of Singar, he was thrown into prison, and, by the order of King Khosrau, he was crucified for having abandoned magism and having become a Christian.

58. — Saint Mur Schoubhalmaran, metropolitan of Karka of Beit-Selouk, who wrote books on monastic life. — This blessed lived at the time of the heretic Gabriel, physician to King Khosrau, and was metropolitan of Karka of Beit Selouk. At that time there were no Catholicos. He wrote numerous works on monastic life. Because of the difficulties he had with the inhabitants of Singar, King Kosrau condemned him to exile and he ended his life there.

59. — Saint Mar Sabarjésus, founder of the monastery of Beit Qôqa, in the country of Adiabene. — His family was from the country of Tirhan, from the village of Awâna. He was educated in his village school, and then came to Adiabene. He saw Saint Jesusabran, the martyr, in the prison of Arbele. He rushed to his chains and kissed them reverently. He received the holy habit from the hands of Jesusabran, then went to the mountain and entered the monastery built near the Great Zab. He saw the holy ascetic Hormizd who lived there and became his disciple and secretary. He gave him a cave in which he lived for twelve years. Saint Jesusyab, metropolitan of Adiabene, who later became Catholicos, went to visit him and they greeted each other. He was delighted to see the numerous congregations of brothers gathered around the saint, and established him as superior. He had up to fifty disciples, and he decorated his monastery with all kinds of ornaments. He died on the first day of the great fast, and was buried in the martyrdom which he had built. May his prayer come to the aid of the poor writer.

60. — The monk Jesusabran, martyr, under whose name a monastery was built in the town of Arbela, and the twelve martyrs his companions. — In the time of King Khosrau, the thirtieth year of his reign, thirteen confessors were seized. The name of the first of them was Jesusabran. For fifteen years, they were loaded with chains in the town of Arbela. They were then taken to the village of Dewarda (?), next to the bridge which separates Beit Garmai from the country of Beleschphar, and there they were crucified. Some followers of Arbele came to take their relics and built a famous monastery in their honor.

61. — Saint Mar Michael, who founded a convent in Diabene, in the neighborhood of the town of Kephar-Ouziel. — This blessed man had been the disciple of Mar Sabarjesus of Beit Qôqa. After he had lived a long time in solitude, grace called him to leave the monastery of Sabarjesus to build another convent in the vicinity of the town of Kephar-Ouziel, in the village of Tar'el, about five stages of the monastery of his spiritual father. He applied himself to works of virtue. He enriched his monastery with books, superb ornaments and goods. He migrated to his Lord in profound old age. His monastery was completed and enlarged by the care of Sabarjesus, son of Nakôr, of the city of Kephar-Oaziel.

62. — Saint Henanjesus, disciple of Mar Sabarjesus of Beit Qôqa. — His family was from Adiabene and his village was called Xahschinvân. He studied the books and their commentaries at the schools in his village. He then came to find Saint Sabarjesus who gave him the holy habit. He remained in a cell for a long time, until his lust was appeased. He became superior of the convent of Beit Qôqa. He migrated to the Lord and his body was placed in martyrdom.

63. — Saint Mar John, superior of the monastery of Beit Qôqa. — His family was from Adiabene. He came to Mar Sabarjesua and received the habit from him. Then he went with his brother to the mountain of Zamar. Later, the disciples of Mar Sabarjesus came to seek him out to make him their superior after [the death of] Henanjesus. He carried out this function for some time and emigrated to Our Lord.

64. — Saint Schoubhalmaran, superior of the convent of Beit Qôqa. — He was from the country of Ma'alta. He went to the convent of Mar Sabarjésus and received the habit. He spent thirty years in complete solitude. He succeeded Mar John and performed wonders like the Apostles. After having been superior for thirty-five years, he emigrated to his Master, and was placed in martyrdom.

65. — Blessed Mar Joseph, superior of the convent of Beit Qôqa. — His family was from the country of Marga, and his village was called Gaphita. After studying the books, he took up the habit. Until his death he ate nothing cooked. He lived in the mountains for a while. He suffered a short illness and emigrated to Our Lord. He was placed with the Fathers in martyrdom.

66. — Saint Mar Nataniel. superior of the monastery of Beit-Qoqa, and was from the country of Marga, and his village [...] interpreter, martyr, bishop of Siarouzour, who commented on David, wrote against the wise men. — He was from the country of Siarouzour and went to the schools of Nisibis where he learned the doctrine; then he wrote a polemical treatise against the Magi, and a commentary on the psalms. He then became bishop of Scheharzour. King Khosrau used the cruellest tortures against him and ended up having him crucified. The faithful placed him in his cathedral church.

67. — Saint Abba Simeon who founded the monastery of the city Schênâ. — His family was from Beit Aramayè, from the country of Kaschkar. Before taking the monastic habit, he crossed the Tigris. He went to find Rabban Bar-Idta, who founded a convent in the country of Marga and received the monastic habit from him. He lived in solitude in this convent, and then went to Jerusalem where he spent a long time. Then he returned and lived alone in the mountain of Beit Nineveh. Brothers gathered near him, and he built a beautiful temple. He became superior in the monastery of Mar Ganiba, in the neighborhood of Karka-de-Beit-Selouk. Saint Rabban Afnimaran, who founded the monastery of Beit-Nouhadra, was led by Mar Simeon. He died and was buried in the convent of Mar Çeliba near the Çarçar river. Two years after his death he was taken away and transported to the town of Schena, and he was placed in his monastery.

68. — Saint Mar Habiba, superior of the Great Convent of Ida. His family was from the country of Beit-Nouhadra. He was raised by Rabban Dadjesus, leader of the Great Monastery. He went to the Lord at ninety-two years old and left this world and was deposited in the Martyrion.

69. — Saint Abba Zinai, who is said to have founded the monastery house in Adiabene— After having studied the books sufficiently, he came to find a certain famous monk who lived in a monastery in Adiabene and was called Etienne. He received the habit from him. When this holy man died. Abba Zinai, [...] at the foot of the mountain, it was built in the surroundings of the monastery and a convent. Then he went to find Mar Babai of Xisibe, as well as Saint Rabban Ebedjesus, his companion: and they spent some time together. More than sixty brothers gathered around him. Ivory adorned the monastery with all kinds of decorations, he went to the Lord, and his body was placed in

the church. It was placed in the monastery in the hands of Saint Mar Bar-Schabta who himself left a few years later and founded a convent in the country of Ma'alta and Henaitha.

70. — Saint Mar Ebedjesus, disciple of Mar Babai of Nisbis. He was from the country of Schaharaour; his parents were noble. He went to Mar Babai and placed himself in his direction. When Mar Babai went to live in the mountain of Adiabene and then returned to find a monastery on Mount Izla. He lived forty-nine years and emigrated to the Lord. He was placed in the church, opposite Mar Babai.

71. — Saint Mar Simeon, who founded the Beit-Bagasch monastery. — When [...] entirely [...] of Mar Yônan, in the surroundings of the village of Ashgar, and he practiced asceticism there for some time. Then he left the convent and went to the mountain of Beit-Bagascli, where he lived in a cave. He built cells and a church and taught many disciples. At the age of seventy he emigrated to Our Lord, and his body was placed in the monastery which he had built. — Saint Rabban Mar Narsai, superior of the monastery of Mar Abraham the Great, in Ida. — His carnal family was from the country of Kaschkar. He studied the books and their commentaries and made his novitiate in the Grand Convent. On the night of the Passion, he went to Jerusalem and returned that same night. He left his temporary life, and at the age of ninety-six years emigrated to Our Lord; his body was placed in the martyrion.

73. — Saint Mar Theodore, who founded a school in the country of Kaschkar. — He was from the country of Kaschkar. He went to Mar Babai of Nisibis, received the habit from him and returned to his country. He built a large monastery there, in which he established a hsopital and a school. Saint Mar Makika who founded the convent of Beit-Nischar was directed by him. After enjoying a good old age, he emigrated to Our Lord and was deposited in the school that he had built.

74. — Saint Mar Babai, the scribe, who wrote a book on monastic life. — He was from the country of Beit Qardou, and went to the city of Hirta. He became scribe of the marzban of Hirta. One day he went out with the marzban to go hunting; and it pleased God to take Mar Babai himself. He arrived by chance at a cave in the Hirta desert where he found a monk. He entered near him who

instructed him in the practice of virtue and gave him the holy habit. He remained close to him for a long time and wrote books on monastic life. He prophesied about the desert of Beit-Hale and about Rabban Koudâhwi, its founder. There was once a dissension in the city of Hirta, concerning faith. The locals came to get him and took him away. The bishop said to him: "Lead the people who have placed their called Qancea". He turned to a little child who had never spoken and said to him: "Child, why are you baptized?" And the child, hitherto deprived of speech, replied: "I am baptized in the name of the Father, and of the Pila, and of the Holy Spirit, and I confess that Christ is God and perfect man." Then the saint said to them: "Here is the holy and true confession". When he returned to Our Lord, he ordered -Mar Abba 'Abda to place him in his cave. Later a monastery was built above.

75. — Saint Mur 'Abda, from the monastery of Me'are. — His family was from Beit-Aramayê, near the town of Aqoula, near Hirta. He was a mage. One day he went to the monastery of Mar Serguis. It was Saturday, the eve of Resurrection Sunday. A large crowd was in this monastery that day. He saw a light which illuminated the baptized. He went to schools and studied books; then he went to Mar Babai the Scribe who gave him the holy habit. He stayed near him for some time. When he wanted to leave, he had a dream in which [God] said: "Do not go; behold, a man from Hirta [is] coming to you: change his name and call him Mar Abda. He is destined to receive great revelations." His dream came true. When he died, Mar Abda the Younger, his disciple, placed him in his cave and built a convent above it which is still called today- the Convent of Abba Mar Abda.

76. — Saint Mar Abda the Younger Bar-Hotif, disciple of Abba Mar Abda, founder of the convent of Me'are. — His carnal family was from the city of Hirta, and one of the noblest. He did not ever think of becoming a monk and his vocation came from God Mar 'Abda [the Elder] was about to breathe his last when an angel of the Lord said to him: "Here I am to you. bring a young man from Hirta. He will relieve you with his services. Change his name and call him Mar 'Abda of your own name. — And this angel said [to the young man]: "Go, become a monk, and put yourself in the service of the old man Mar Abda". The angel appeared to him three times. He came to find Mar Abda, received it from him and served it until his death. He made many conversions

among the pagans. During his time the convent of Beit Hâlè was built. He lived for a hundred years and emigrated to Our Lord.

77. — Saint Rabban Bar-Sahdê, who founded a monastery in the village of Barouqa (?), in the surroundings of the monastery of Gamrê (?). — His family was from the town of Dêrin which is on an island in the Qatarayê Sea. He was going down with the merchants, by sea, to the country of India. In one of these voyages they were surprised by pirates who killed those who were with them on the ship. He then made this vow: "If I escape, I will become a monk." None of those in the ship escaped except him. He then went to the monastery of Rabban Schabhour who gave him the habit; then he came to Rabban 'Abda and made himself his disciple. Later, he retired into solitude in the vicinity of the village of Barouqa (?). He built a monastery and brothers gathered near him. He gave up his spirit to Our Lord and was placed in the church he had built.

78. — Saint Mar Koudâhwi, who founded the monastery of Beit-Hale. — His family was from Beit-Aramayê. After attending school, he went to find Saint Rabban Abba Schabhour, who had founded a monastery in the mountain of Schischtarin, town of Beit Houzayê. He received the holy habit from him and devoted himself to asceticism in a cell for some time. He then went to the desert of Hirta, and lived there in a cave. He built a monastery in the desert of Beit Hâlê. At the age of ninety-five, he came to Our Lord and his body was placed under the portico of the church.

79. — Mar Schoubhalmaran, an ascetic, founded a monastery in the mountain of Masabadan. — His family was from Beit-Aramayê. He went to find Rabban Koudâhwi, founder of the monastery of Beit Hâlê, and received the habit from him. He lived for a while in the mountains, in solitude, then brothers gathered near him and he built a monastery. He died and was buried in this monastery.

80. — Mar Serguis Daouda, who founded a monastery in the mountain of Kaschkar. — His family was from Beit Aramayê, from the country of Kaschkar. He received the monastic habit in the monastery of Rabban Koudâhwi, and lived there for a long time in solitude. He built a monastery in his country of Kaschkar. At the age of one hundred and ten years he emigrated to Our Lord and was placed in the church which he had built.

81. — Blessed Schcubhalmaran, who founded a monastery near Schabrog (?) of Beit-Garmai. — His family was from Beit-Aramayè. He went to the convent of Rabban Koudâhwi, of Beit Hâlê, and put on the habit. Two brothers joined him: Basil and Shila. He became doorman of the monastery; then he devoted himself for some time to asceticism in solitude. He received orders from God to build a monastery on the banks of the Schabroud (?) River in Beit Garmai. Seventy men gathered around him. He left this world in a happy old age and left the monastery to Blessed Basil. His body was placed in the martyrion that he had built.

82. — Blessed Dadjesus hastened a monastery. — His family was from Mahozê-Badaroun, a town near Baghdad. He went to the monastery of Beit-Hâlê and received the habit from the hands of the superior of the convent, Mar Babai, a disciple of Rabban Koudhâwi. He lived for some time in a cell, then he built a monastery in the vicinity of the town of Hirta. He died in a happy old age and was placed in this monastery.

83. — Blessed Mar Abraham, who restored, with Mar Dadjêsus, the monastery of Qâqi near the village of Badaroun in the neighborhood of Bagdad and made it a convent. — His family was from Beit Aramayê. He went to the monastery of Beit Hâlè and put on the habit. He attached himself to John Azraq who subsequently became bishop of Hirta. He remained for some time in a cell, then he left the monastery with ten brothers who attached themselves to him and went to Mahôzé-Badaroun, on the bank of the Tigris. The faithful chose him as director with Mar Dadjêsus. He restored the monastery of Qâqî (?) and made it a magnificent convent. He had around ninety brothers. He emigrated to Our Lord and was deposited in the monastery.

84. — Blessed Mar Ezekiel, who founded a monastery in Beit Garmai. — Mar Ezekiel was born on the same day as Emperor Constantine. He was from the city of Egypt, from the tribe of Manasseh, son of Joseph. He received the coat from the hands of Mar Eugene. He died on the first Friday of Advent, the sixth of first of Kanun. There were sixteen hundred and fifty-two monks in his monastery.

85. — Saint Mar Dausa, who founded a monastery in Beit Aramayê, in the vicinity of the town of Beit Àschkaphïl, which is still called today the monastery of Bar-Haziz. — His family was from the country of Kaschkar He went, with another individual named John, to the monastery of Rabban Koudâhwi and received the habit. He remained for some time in a cell; then he left the monastery with John, and they came together near the village of Aschkaphil, the neighborhood of Doura Qounî. They built a monastery, and brothers gathered near them. After enjoying a happy old age, he emigrated to his Lord and his body was placed in the monastery which he had built.

86. — Blessedar Babai, a Persian, superior of a monastery. — He was the disciple of Rabban Koudâhwi and took the habit. When Rabban Coudahwi died he designed it for his successor. He himself died and was buried in the monastery.

87. — Blessed Mar David Bar-Noutara, who founded a monastery in the neighborhood of Merw, town of Korasan. — His family was from Merw. He went to the monastery of Rabban Koudâhwi and took the habit. Then he returned to his country and built a superb monastery. After enjoying a happy old age, he emigrated to Our Lord, and his body was placed in the temple that he had built.

88. — Saint Rabban Hormizd, who built a monastery in the mountain of the town of Beit Adrai. — He was of Persian origin. After studying the books, he went to the monastery of Rabban Bar-Idta and put on the habit. For years, he practiced asceticism in a cell, and stayed with Rabban Yôzédeq in the convent of Rischa, which is in the mountain of Beit Nouhadra. Later, he went to the mountain of Beit 'Adrai, in the vicinity of the village of Alqosch, and he built a monastery there. At the age of ninety, he emigrated to Our Lord and his body was placed in the martyrdom that he had built.

89. — Saint Rabban Qamjesus, who founded a convent in the mountain of Heftoun, near Marga. — He was from the country of Marga, from the village of Couf. He went to find Mar Jacob of Beit 'Abe. He gave the holy habit to Bar-Sahdè, that is to say Mar Tyris, who had attached himself to him, and both then went to the mountain of Ourouk, where they lived for some time in solitude; then they returned to Beit 'Abè, where Qamjesus was made superior.

He abandoned his charge and went to live in the mountain of Heftoun, about ten miles from Beit-Abè. He then built a monastery in this place; and, in a happy old age, he went to Our Lord. His body was placed in his monastery.

90. — Saint Mar Yâzédeq, who founded a monastery in the Qardou mountains. — He was from the country of Nineveh, from the village called Beit Scliamina. After studying the books, he went to the monastery of Rabban Bar-'Idta, in the country of Marga, and received the monastic habit. He lived in the familiarity of Rabban Hormizd, who founded a monastery in the mountain of Alkosch, and of Abba Simeon, who founded one in the mountain of Shena. He left the convent and went to live for a while in the Rischa monastery. He had a revelation and went to the country of Qardou, where he built a famous convent. Brothers gathered around him. He left this world at the age of eighty and was buried in the temple he had built.

91. — Saint Mar Jesusabran, superior of the monastery that Bahban Yôzédeq had founded in the Qardou mountains. — His family was from the country of Nouhadra. After studying the books, he went to Mar Yôzédeq and led a common life for seven years, according to the rule established by Rabban Yôzédeq in his monastery. He then lived in solitude and became superior of the monastery. He emigrated to Our Lord and was deposited in the convent of his master.

92. — Saint Mar Sabarjesus, metropolitan of Beit Garmai. — His family was from Beit Aramayê. He studied books in the land of Radan. The catholicos Mar Sabarjésus made him reader in his own monastery of Beit Garmai, where he remained for some time. He then left and went to the mountain of Sche'ran, to live in solitude in his master's cave. When the plague ravaged Beit Garmai, he prayed, and the plague was stopped. He built a large monastery in the place called Babta-Mahôzê, which is located in the mountain of Bascheran. He left this world and was placed in the monastery he had built. He had received the imposition of the hands of Catholicos Mar Ameh, in his capacity as metropolitan of Beit-Garmay.

93. — Saint Mm-Afnimaran, who founded a monastery in the mountain of Beit Nouhadra. — His family was from Karka of Beit-Lorsk. He went to find Abba Siméon who founded a convent in the town of Schena. He advised him

to go to Beit-Abê, and he followed this advice. He received the habit of Rabban Qamjésus, Superior of the convent of Beit-Abê. After leading a common life, he lived for a time in deep solitude, then went to the monastery of Zarnouqa where he remained for three years. He left there with brothers who had attached themselves to him and came to the monastery of Mar John of Halhalah. It was known as a magnificent convent; but he aroused jealousy; he left and lived in solitude in the place where Saint Gousjesus the anchorite had lived, at the foot of the mountain. He built a famous monastery there and brothers gathered around him. He left his temporary life at the age of a hundred and was placed in the martyrion he had built.

94. — Saint Mar Georges. — He was from the family of Jesusabran the martyr. He spent some time in the convent of Mar Yôzédeq. At the age of ninety he emigrated to Our Lord, and his body was placed in martyrdom.

95. — Saint Mar Makika, hermit of the convent of Beit Nischar. — After studying the books, he went to Jerusalem. His family was from Kaschkar. He came to the convent of Beit Nischar and lived in deep solitude. He emigrated to Our Lord, and they placed him in the monastery.

96. — The blessed Rabban Abraham, who founded a monastery in Dasen. — His family was from the country of Kaschkar. He went to Beit-Abê, received the habit and remained for some time in a cell. He was pushed by God to go to the country of Dasen and build a convent there. So he left Beit-Abê with saint Mar Zekajesus who had attached himself to him, and went to live in the solitude of the mountain. He built a convent, and about forty brothers gathered near it. At this time, the Catholics Mar Georges went up to the country of Marga and forced Mar Abraham to accept the episcopate of Dasen. He preached extensively. When he abdicated the episcopate, he returned to Beit 'Abè, and remained for some time in a cell. He died and was laid at the feet of Mar Jacob.

97. — Blessed Abba Salomon, superior of the monastery of Mar Jèsusyab of Beit Nouhadra. — His family was from the country of Adiabene. He went to the monastery of Mar Sabarjesus of 'Aba Schapîra and took the holy habit. He was forced to become superior of the convent of Mar Jèsusyab. He held this

office for some time; then he died and was placed at the feet of Mar Jèsusyab and Mar Jacob.

98. — Babban Mélekjésus, from the New Monastery of Elam. — His family was from Beit-Houzayê. He studied the books and received the habit of Shabhour, whose disciple he became. He built a convent in the desert of Elam, at the foot of the mountain. Brothers gathered around him. He died and was buried in his convent.

99. — Blessed Pethion, disciple of Rabban Afnimaran the Great. — His family was from the village of Basoum, in Beit Garmai. He was raised under the eyes of Rabban Afnimaran, and he took the habit. He became superior of the Small Convent. He died and forbade his history to be written. His body was placed at the feet of Mar Afnimaran.

100. — Saint Babban George, who founded a convent in the country of Terse, in the neighborhood of the town of Astahr. — As a child, he studied at the schools of Kaschkar, his hometown. He went to the hermit Makika, received the habit from him and lived under his direction for some time. He then went to the mountains of Persia and built a convent in the city of Astahr. Brothers gathered near him. He emigrated to our Lord and was deposited in the monastery which he had built.

101. — Abba Çeliba, who founded the monastery of Beit Nouhadrâ. — His family was from the country of Adiabene. He had four fleshly brothers who were monks. His village was Beit-Caidahe re[...] received the habit and attached himself to it for some time. Then he went to the mountain of Beit Nouhadra, to the place called Beit-Asya. He built a superb convent in this place. About fifty brothers gathered around him. He gathered the brothers near him and appointed Rabban Cyriacus the Great as superior, who subsequently became bishop of Balad. He emigrated to Our Lord at the age of eighty, on Thursday of the week of the Dedication of the Church.

102. — Blessed Cyriacus, disciple of Ahba Çeliba and bishop of Balad. — He was from Doura Arabaya, a Christian village in the country of Tirhan. He went to Beit-Arabayè, near Saint Kabban Ba'outh who gave him the habit. Then he came to the mountain of Zinai, where he remained for some time; then he went

to the Qardou mountains, where he settled in the vicinity of the monastery of Kamoul. Later he came to live near Abba Çeliba, whose disciple he became. One hundred and thirty brothers were gathered around them. Subsequently, the people of Balad came with an edict from Mar Cyprianus of Nisibus and took him to make him their bishop. He left the monastery in the hands of Saint Mar Atqen. He was consecrated a bishop. He redoubled his labors and built a magnificent cathedral church. After governing his diocese for thirteen years, he emigrated to Our Lord and his body was placed in the large church that he had built.

103. — Saint Rabban Ba'outh, of the monastery of Mar Yônan of Uar-Toitra, who founded a monastery in the country of Beit Nohadra. — His family was from Beit 'Arabayê. He received the habit from the hands of Mar Yônan de Bar-Toura, and lived for some time in seclusion. He had a dream: "You will sleep with a mother and her daughter." He made his dream known to Mar Jesusabran, the beloved disciple of Mar John of Dailam, who answered him: "Christ made me know that you must go to the monastery which is located next to Beit Nouhadra to transform it into a magnificent convent. You will leave this world and you will be buried with the blessed Kouhadokt and her daughter, who in times past laid the foundations of this monastery". — So he left the monastery of Bar-Toura and went to transform the monastery into a convent. When he emigrated to Our Lord, his body was placed at the feet of the saints, and thus the prophecy of Jesusabran was fulfilled.

104. — Saint Jesusabran, companion of Mar John of Dailam. — His family was from Beit Garmai. After studying the books, he went to Saint Abba Simeon of Kaschkar, who had founded a monastery in the mountain of Shena, and he received from him the monastic habit. At that time, Saint Abba Simeon was superior of the convent of Mar Ganiba, in Beit Garmai. Mar Jesusabran left the monastery of Mar Ganiba and went to the mountain of Beit Bagasch where he found Mar John of Dailam with Abraham Sanouta his master, and he lived near them in a cave. After some time, the three of them came to the desert of Beit Gaza, and he lived in solitude. There appeared in the country of Adiabene a troop of bandits from the country of Dailam who seized Saint Jesusabran and Mar John of Dailam, and took them captive, each on their own. Jesusabran was shepherd of the flocks of the one who had seized him. Subsequently, he healed his master's son from a serious illness who freed him. After reaching a profound

THE BOOK OF THE CHASTE

old age, he emigrated to Our Lord and his body was placed at the feet of Abba Yônan of BarToura.

105. — **The blessed Abba Dairata, disciple of Afnimaran the Great.** — His family was from Beit Garmai, and he received the habit of Âbba Siméon, founder of the convent of Schena, while the latter was superior of the convent of Mar Ganiba, in the country of Beit Garmai. Then, he went to the convent of Beit Abè and attached himself to Saint Afnimaran, who founded a convent - Luis the mountain of Beit Nouhadra. He left Beit 'Abê, as did Rabban Afnimaran, and he came to the convent built by the latter where he devoted himself to asceticism for some time. After having accomplished many works, he emigrated to Our Lord and was placed at the feet of Afnimaran.

106. — **Holy Wall Abraham of Me'arê, who built the course of Mar Eugene.** — His family was from the village of Me'arê. He received the habit from the hands of Mar Abraham who built [a convent] on the summit of the mountain of Beit Nouhadra. He remained for some time in the convent of Rischa, and then Mar Abraham sent him to the convent of Mount Izla. He repaired the ruins of the convent of Mar Eugène. About fifty men gathered around him. He fell ill, called his spiritual sons and said to them: "Behold, after my death, Rouzbîhân will come from the convent of Mar Michael of Mosul; he will be your superior". And he emigrated to Our Lord, and his body was laid to rest. in the martyrdom of the convent.

107. — **Saint Rouzbîhdn, metropolitan of Nisibis.** — His family was from the town of Nisibis. He went to the small monastery of Mar Michael in Mosul. He received the habit of Mar Jésusyab, superior of the monastery, nephew through his mother of the Catholicos Mar Celibazeka. He remained for some time in this place, and then went to the monastery of Mar Eugene, after the death of the superior, Mar Abraham, as the latter had prophesied. Sometime later he was appointed Metropolitan of Nisibis. He gave a village called Hizgan, to the monastery of Mar Eugene. Then he emigrated to Our Lord and his body was placed in the church of Nisibis.

108. — **Saint Mar Zokê, bishop of Hadeth.** — His family was from Beit Garmai. He went to the convent of Aba Schapîra, after having received the habit in the convent of Kabban Basîma, in the country of Qardou. He attached

himself to Saint Afnimaran the Great. He was canonically instituted bishop of the city of Hadeth. He performed many signs and wonders. He emigrated to Our Lord, and his body was placed in the martyrion of the great church (cathedral).

109. — Saint Kabban Safra, who founded a monastery on Mount Izla. — He was from Mesopotamia. He received the habit in the convent of Mar Eugène and lived in solitude until the death of his master. He then moved two steps away from the monastery and built one himself. Monks gathered around him. After reaching his old age, he emigrated to Our Lord and his body was placed in the convent that he had built.

110. — Saint Abba Joseph, who built a convent opposite the town of Balad. — He was from the country of Shahrazour, and he went to the convent of Beit-Abê, where he took the habit. He devoted himself to asceticism with ardor and governed the convent for years. When the Catholicos Celibazeka went to the convent, Joseph resigned from his charge, left there and came to the desert on the bank of the Tigris, in the neighborhood of the town of Balad. There were two brothers there; he built a famous convent there; he gave his instructions to the brothers about this convent and emigrated to Our Lord.

111. — Saint Abba Jesus, superior of the convent, disciple of Habban Afnimaran. — His family was from Awâna in the Tirhan. He taught in the schools and went to find Afnimaran. He took the habit, and devoted himself to asceticism in solitude. He came to the convent of Âbba Joseph, near Balad, and ended his life there. He was placed at the feet of Rabban Afnimaran and Rabban Pethion.

112. — Blessed Mar John, who built a convent in the country of Qardou. — He was of Persian origin. He received the habit in the monastery of Rabban Bar-Idta of Marga, and practiced asceticism there for a time. Then he left the convent and went to live in a cave in the Qardou munis. He built a magnificent church in the vicinity of the village of Dadar. He lived in this place until the end of his life, and he was placed in his convent.

113. — Blessed Siméon, superior of the monastery of Rabban Yôzèdeq. — He was from the village of Marga, located in the region of the Qardou mountains.

He was educated in the monastery of Mar Adôna, in the country of Qardou. This Adôna was from Kaschkar, in Beit Aramayè; he became metropolitan of 'Elam and received the crown of martyrdom under King Shapor. His relics were transported to the region of Qardou and the school was built above [his tomb]. in which Max Siméon was raised. The latter went to find Mar Jesusabran, disciple of Rabban Yôzédeq, who gave him the habit. He lived for some time in a cell and became superior of the convent of Mar Yôzédeq. He emigrated to Our Lord and. was deposited in this convent.

114. — The blessed Rabban Joseph, who founded a monastery in the country of Beit-Nouhadra. — He was from the country of Dasen. He went to find Rabban Jacob who lived in a cave. He gave him the habit. He studied the doctrine and devoted himself for some time to asceticism. He built a superb church. When Mar Jacob went to the convent of Mar Jésusyab, and came to the mountain of Beit-Nouhadra, Rabban Joseph stayed with him in this convent, and they ended their lives there.

115. — Saint Abba Bar-Daira, anchorite. — His village, located in the country of Qardou, was called Scheban. He studied at the schools, then went to see Cyriacus, superior of the monastery of Abba Celiba, who later became bishop of Balad. He gave him the habit. He devoted himself to asceticism with ardor and lived in the Qardou mountains. He was oppressed by famine, and a marten brought and placed before him twelve acorns. Another time, having smelled something burning, he went out to the door, saw a large grasshopper on the fire, and ate it. For twenty days God thus prepared for him daily a large locust for his food. He then came to the convent of Rabban Afnimaran in Beit Nouhadra; he died there and was buried there.

116. — Saint John of Dailam, who founded a monastery in the mountains of Persia, in the vicinity of the city of Argon. — He was from the city of Hadeth and he was taken captive to their country by the people of Dailam. He built two convents. He died and was placed in the Syrian convent.

117- — Abba Âaron, who founded a monastery called the Convent of the Holy Cross, in the vicinity of the town of Balad. — He was from Awana, in Tirhan. He studied books near Mar Jacob Hazzaya, and he came to the convent of Saint Mar Jésusyab, which is located in the country of Beit-Nouhadra. There he devoted himself to asceticism until the death of Mar Jacob who had given him the habit. At the instigation of Mar Cyriacus, bishop of Balad, and by the care of Aharon, a monastery was built under the name of the precious Wood of the Holy Cross, and it is still called today Convent of the Holy Cross, founded by Abba Aaron. He died and his body was placed in this convent.

118. — Mar Béktjesus, who founded at the foot of the mountain of Sinai a convent which is called the convent of Marga. — He was from Adiabène, from the village called Qatarta-Zab. He went to the convent located next to little Zab and called the Schinerô convent. There he took the habit and practiced asceticism with ardor. He then went to live for a while in the mountain of Zinai. When he became old, he went down to stay in the village of Zinai. in the place called Margana, where Saint Mar Niha had once dwelt. Brothers gathered around him and he built a convent and cells. He fell asleep in the Lord and his body was placed in the martyrdom that he had built.

119. — The blessed Mar Aiqen, who built a convent in the mountain of Beit-Nouhadra. — He was from Beit Garmai; After studying the doctrine, he went to the convent of Mar Abraham the Great. He received the habit and devoted himself to asceticism with ardor. Then, he went to live on the mountain of Beit-Nouhadra, in the vicinity of the convent of Abba Celiba. He built a magnificent convent there and gathered brothers around him. He died and was buried in this convent.

120. — The blessed Mar Abraham, who founded a center in the vicinity of the city of Hitli, on the bank of the Euphrates. — He was from Beit-Aramayè. He took the habit in the convent of Beit-Hâlè and went to the monastery of Gamrè where he devoted himself to asceticism. He was chosen to be superior of the convent of Barouqa, located in the vicinity of that of Gamrè. Later he came to the town of Hîth, in Beit-Aramayè, where he built a convent and cells on the bank of the Euphrates. Brothers gathered around him. He died in a happy old age and was placed in his convent.

121. — Blessed Mar Gabriel of Kaschkar, who founded three monvents: the first in the surroundings of Maliozê de Ariiran, in Beit Garmai; I second around Doura-Qouni: and the third, which is called convent of Gàbbârê, in the country of Beit BouscJimê. — He was from Beit Aramayê. He built a

monastery outside his village; he gathered some brothers there, then he left for Jerusalem. He took the habit in a convent, located next to Çaidîn, which had been founded by a holy personage from the country of Kaschkar. He devoted himself to asceticism there, then he returned to the country of Kaschkar in Doura de Qouni, and he built near the village of Karsa a convent which is still called today convent of Karsa. to two hundred brothers in this convent Shortly after, he went to the country of Beit Rouschmê, near the country of Kaschkar, and built in the surroundings of the village called Houçaraya, a convent which is still called today the convent of Gabbârê. This blessed also built the convent of Mar Gabriel in Mosul. He died in a monastery in Beit Garmai, in the year one thousand and fifty of the Greeks. His body was taken away and placed in his convent. Later Mahôzè was devastated, and the convent was destroyed fifty-nine years after the death of Mar Gabriel. The brothers of the Karsa monastery took care of his body and placed it in front of the church.

122. — Blessed Henanjesus, (who built the convent of Beit-Reqna, near the city of Hadeth. — His family was from Adiabene. He took the habit and came to the city of Hadeth, where he built a convent under the name of Mar John the Evangelist, He was helped in this construction by the people of the tribe called Beit-Reqna, and the convent is still called Convent of Beit-Reqna. He died, and his spiritual sons. placed him under the peristyle of the church he had built.

123. — Saint Abba Schamascha, who built a convent in Beit Ammayê, in the surroundings of the city of Anbar, near a village called Uewab (?). — He was from Beit Aramayè. He was a disciple of Saint Rabban Mar Abda, and practiced asceticism under his direction. Then he went for some time to the mountain of the Assyrians and came to the neighborhood of Anbar. He built a convent and gathered brothers around him. He fell asleep in the Lord and was placed in his convent.

124. — Saint Mar Isaac, of Nineveh, who abdicated his bishopric and wrote books on monastic life. — He was created bishop of Nineveh by the Catholicos Mar Georges, in the monastery of Beit 'Abè. After having governed the diocese of Nineveh for five months, as successor to Bishop Moses, he abdicated the episcopate for reasons known to God, and went to live in the mountains. The seat remained vacant for some time; then his successor was Mar Sabarjesus, who

himself abdicated the episcopate, lived as an anchorite in the time of the Catholicos Henanjesus, and died in the monastery of Mar Schahin, in the country of Qardou. Isaac, after having left the seat of Nineveh, went to the mountain of Matout which surrounds the country of Beit Houzayê, and dwelt in solitude with the anchorites who were there. He then came to the convent of Rabban Schabhour. He was very devoted to the study of holy books, to the point that he lost his sight as a result of his dedication to reading and his abstinence. He was well versed in the knowledge of the divine mysteries; he wrote admirable works on monastic life. He wrote three proposals which were not accepted by many people. Daniel Bar Toubanitha, bishop of Beit Garmai, spoke out against him because of the things he had said. He left his temporary life in profound old age, and his body was placed in the monastery of Schabhour. As he was from Beit Qatarayè, I think that jealousy aroused the people of Mesopotamia, as well as against Joseph Hazzaya, John of Apamea and John of Dilaita.

125. — Saint Abba Joseph Hazzaya, also called 'Ebedjesus. — He was of Persian origin; his city was called Nemroud. His father was a mage, and he himself was leader of the Mages. When Omar Ibn Hatibeut took the reins of the empire of the Arabs, and he sent his troops to fight against the Turks, the city of Nemroud, founded by Nimrod, who called it by his name, revolted against him and did not open its doors to him. Joseph, who was found outside the gate, was taken captive with one hundred and thirty people. He was seven years old when he was taken. An Arab from the town of Singar bought him for three hundred and seventy zouzê, circumcised him with his children, and made him a pagan. He stayed with this man for three years. Then his master died, and his children sold him to a Christian named Cyriacus, from the village of Dadar, in the country of Qardou, for five hundred and seventy zouzê. This man took him with him to his house where he made him steward, because he had no son. Cyriacus strongly urged him to become a Christian; but he would not allow himself to be persuaded. He took him with him to the monastery of Kamoul, which was in the vicinity of the village, and the young man, seeing the monks, was excited by the love of Our Lord and received baptism in the monastery of Mar John of Kamoul. Cyriacus freed him when he saw that he was diligent in prayer and had the desire to become a monk. He then left for the monastery of Abba Celiba, in the country of Beit Nouhadra. He was received by Blessed Cyriacus, superior of the monastery, who subsequently became bishop of

Balad. He practiced common life and applied himself especially to the reading of psalms and holy books. Then he went to the land of Qardou and dwelt in the place called Araba. He stayed there for many years. Then the faithful came to seek him out to make him superior to the monastery of Mar Basima, in the country of Urdu. He governed this monastery for a while, then went to the mountain of Sinai. He remained there for a certain time, and, at the instigation of Mar Koudahwi, bishop of Hirta, the faithful made him superior of the convent of Rabbau Boktiesus, nicknamed of 'Margana', which was located in the vicinity of the village of Sinai. never stopped composing books. He had a physical brother called Ebedjesus. He came from the city of Nemroud, received baptism and became a monk. Since then, he wrote all his books under his name. brother Ebedjesus. He wrote in his works four passages, which were not approved by the doctors of the Church. Mar Timothy held a synod and anathematized it, the year one hundred and seventy of the reign of the sons of Hischam. Did he draw his doctrine? We can learn it from his story written by Mar. He died in profound old age and the brothers buried him in the convent of Rabban Mar Atqen, waiting for the Lord to come and resurrect him. May his prayers and the prayers of all the saints who are mentioned in this book be a protective wall for the poor person who owns it and for his parents. Amen.

126. — Saint Mur John, who founded a monastery in the country of Qardou and lived in the mountain of Beit Dilaita. — He was from the country of Beit Nouhadra, and he read all the books in the schools. He took the habit in the monastery of Mar Yôzédeq and attached himself to blessed Stephen, disciple of Mar Jacob Hazzaya and Rabban Afnimaran. John had two physical brothers: Serguis and Theodoros, who also became monks. He left the convent to live in the mountain of Beit Dilaita, where his food was wild blackberries instead of bread. He wrote numerous works on monastic life. Later, he came to live in the Qardou mountains, near the village of Argoul. Brothers gathered around him and he built a monastery. The books he composed were not approved by Catholicos Timothy who convened a synod and anathematized him for having said in his work that the humanity of Our Lord is united to his divinity. Having reached a great old age, he gathered the faithful and the monks and gave them his instructions regarding the monasteries. At the same time, he emigrated to Our Lord and his body was placed in the convent of Sahdôna.

127. — **The bishop of Mahozê of Ariwan, Mar Tyris also called Bar-Sahdê.** — He was from the country of Beit Nouhadra, from the village of Halamoun. He was raised in the school of Mar Aitallaha. Having learned that Mar Jacob had left the monastery of Mar Abraham, on Mount Izla, and was beginning to build a convent in the country of Marga, he came to him and placed himself under his direction. Blessed Qamjesus, who in his old age built a monastery on the summit of the mountain of Heftoun, came to join him. Mar Jacques gave them the habit; he appointed Qamjesus to build the convent and made Mar Tyris its steward. He devoted himself to asceticism and lived in solitude. He wrote books on monastic life, and Jesusyab of Arbèle established him bishop of Mahozê of Ariwan in Beit Garmai. He departed from the Orthodox faith. When Jesusyab, metropolitan of Adiabene, learned of this, as he had affection for him, he wrote to him: "Abandon your opinion". But he did not allow himself to be persuaded by the words of Mar Jesusyab. The Fathers assembled near the Catholicos Mar Ameh, and anathematized him, tore up his profession of faith, and established Mar Saba as bishop in his place. He therefore went to live in the mountains. As he did not find peace of conscience, he returned promptly to Mar Sabarjesus, metropolitan of Beit Garmai, and confessed his brother. But he did not persevere in this feeling. He went to the emperor of the Romans, Heraclius, who was then in Jerusalem, and he said to him: "I am persecuted by the Eastern bishops because I profess the true faith." And he made his profession of faith in the church, and anathematized the saints' supporters of Diodorus Then, on the order of the emperor, he was appointed bishop of Edessa. He governed the diocese of Edessa for a short time, because his apostasy did not benefit him. the emperor and he affirmed that he professed the opinions of Diodorus. On the orders of the emperor, he was expelled from Edessa. He then came to the catholicos Mar Ameli and asked him for absolution. ascetic who had practiced virtue, the catholicos Mar Âmeh consented to Sahdôna returning to his seat, because the blessed Mar Saba was dead. When Mar Jesusyab of Arbela learned of this, he wrote to Mar Ameh a letter in which he told him.: "It was Satan who brought Sahdona from the land of the Romans and obviously brought him before you. He has with him two books which he composed against our faith and our belief. When [the Fathers] read this letter, they no longer wanted to admit Mar Tyris Sahdôna into the Church. He did not remain there, but, weeping and groaning, he returned to Edessa and dwelt in a cave in the mountain. It is said that he rejected heretical opinions and converted to the truth. He lived a long time in solitude, and when

he died, he was buried in his cave. After Sahdôna was expelled from the Church, Gabriel, superior of the convent of Beit 'Abè, went to find him in Edessa, as he attests in his writings: "After Sahdôna was expelled from the church, I Gabriel, inflamed with ardent zeal, I went to him in Edessa, I argued with him, and I confounded him."

128. — The faithful Ramwai, who founded a monastery at Kaschkar. — He was from the country of Kaschkar, and he built a famous convent in his country.

129. — The faithful Baqra founded [a monastery] on the Tigris, in the vicinity of Ghebilta.

130. — The faithful Gayan founded a convent in the country of Kaschkar.

131. — The monk Abraham founded a monastery in the country of Masabadan.

132. — The blessed nun Daudai founded a monastery in Hirta, city of the Arabs.

133. — Helena, nun, sister of Simeon, Superior of the convent of Rabban Yôzédeq, in the country of Qardou, remained without [eating] bread from the Saturday of the Rogation of the Ninevites until the Sunday of the Resurrection.

134. — Blessed Adramanag also built a monastery in Hirta.

135. — Mar Abraham, during whose life Mar Jésuzeka, zealot and martyr founded a convent in the country of Imameh.

136. — Mar Gabriel built a monastery in the country of Radan.

137. — Mar John built a convent in the country of Beit-Arnê.

138. — Mar Stephen built a convent in Sagistan.

139. — Saint Mar Jesusyab, who left his country to go found a monastery in the mountain of Beit Nouhadra. — When he was young, he went to the schools of Tamanôn, and studied books there. He left the schools and went to find Mar Jesusyeka in the country of Adiabene. He was a reader in the monastery of Mar Jesus Çeliba Zeka. After some time, Mar Zeka sent him to Mar Babai of Nisibis, and he received the holy habit on Mount Izla. After the death of his master, he came to the mountain of Beit Nouhadra with three other brothers, and he founded a famous monastery there. Brothers gathered near him. Later, Blessed Mar Isaac, bishop of Beit Nouhadra, begged him not to abandon his monastery. He allowed himself to be persuaded by the bishop. After an illustrious life, he emigrated to Our Lord at the age of fifty-six and was laid to rest in the convent he had built.

140. — Saint Mar Jacob, the prophet and seer, disciple of Mar Jésusyàb. — His family was from Beit-Garmai. He studied in the schools of Harbatlîhelal and went to the monastery of Beit-Abè. He received the habit from the hands of Mar Abraham, superior of the monastery, originally from Kaschkar, - disciple of Mar Jacob, founder of Beit-Abè - who later founded a convent in the country of Dasen. He became his disciple and dwelt in solitude. The Catholicos George wanted to ordain him bishop, but he did not consent. Blessed Henanjesus, catholicos, [also wanted to make him metropolitan] of Nisibis, but he did not listen to him. He went to the country of Beit Nouhadra and lived for three years in a cave. Then, Mar Isaac, bishop of Nouhadra, and the faithful came to look for him for the monastery of Mar Jésusyàb. He went with them. There were more than three hundred brothers in this monastery. He built a magnificent church. He emigrated to Our Lord at the age of ninety, and he was laid in martyrdom at the feet of Mar Jésusyàb.

End of the history of these saints, of the monasteries they built, of the countries they inhabited, [written] in abbreviated notices; there are one hundred and forty of them without counting Heléna mentioned above. May their prayer and that of the righteous and the saints obtain for the miserable writer forgiveness of his sins, now and always.

The Scriptorium Project is the work of a small group of lay people of various apostolic churches who are interested in the preservation, transmission, and translation of the works of the early and medieval church. Our efforts are to make the works of the church fathers accessible to anyone who might have an interest in Christian antiquities and the theological, philosophical, and moral writings that have become the bedrock of Western Civilization.

To-date, our releases have pulled from the Greek, Syriac, Georgian, Latin, Armenian, Indo-Persian, Germanic, Nordic, Slavic, Celtic, Ethiopian, and Coptic traditions of Christianity, and have been pulled from sundry local traditions and languages.

www.ingramcontent.com/pod-product-compliance
Lightning Source LLC
LaVergne TN
LVHW061042070526
838201LV00073B/5146